FREAKY TRUE SCIENCE

FREAKY STORIES ABOUT INVENTIONS

BY MICHAEL CANFIELD

 Gareth Stevens
PUBLISHING

Please visit our website, www.garethstevens.com. For a free color catalog of all our high-quality books, call toll free 1-800-542-2595 or fax 1-877-542-2596.

Library of Congress Cataloging-in-Publication Data

Names: Canfield, Michael, 1977- author.
Title: Freaky stories about inventions / Michael Canfield.
Other titles: Freaky true science.
Description: New York : Gareth Stevens Publishing, [2017] | Series: Freaky true science | Includes bibliographical references and index.
Identifiers: LCCN 2016008668 | ISBN 9781482448191 (pbk.) | ISBN 9781482448290 (library bound) | ISBN 9781482448245 (6 pack)
Subjects: LCSH: Inventions–History–Juvenile literature. | Technology–History–Juvenile literature.
Classification: LCC T48 .C325 2017 | DDC 609–dc23
LC record available at http://lccn.loc.gov/2016008668

First Edition

Published in 2017 by
Gareth Stevens Publishing
111 East 14th Street, Suite 349
New York, NY 10003

Copyright © 2017 Gareth Stevens Publishing

Designer: Sarah Liddell
Editor: R   gelhout

Photo credits: Cover, background throughout book STILLFX/Shutterstock.com; cover, p. 1 (   ) Hein Nouwens/Shutterstock.com; cover, p. 1 (flying machine used throu   ook) AKaiser/Shutterstock.com; cover, p. 1 (phonograph) a40757/Shutterstock.com; pp. 5, 7, 9, 11, 13, 15, 17, 19, 21, 23, 25, 27, 29 (hand used throughout) Helena Ohman/Shutterstock.com; pp. 5, 7, 9, 11, 13, 15, 17, 19, 21, 23, 25, 27, 29 (texture throughout) Alex Gontar/Shutterstock.com; p. 4 DEA/A. DAGLI ORTI/Contributor/De Agostini/Getty Images; p. 5 Magnus Manske/Wikimedia Commons; p. 7 EW CHEE GUAN/Shutterstock.com; p. 9 Arad/Wikimedia Commons; p. 11 Fæ/Wikimedia Commons; p. 13 Martin york/Wikimedia Commons; pp. 15 (Caproni flying machine), 19 General Photographic Agency/Stringer/Hulton Archive/Getty Images; p. 15 (Da Vinci) Stock Montage/Contributor/Archive Photos/Getty Images; p. 16 Yomangani/Wikimedia Commons; p. 17 (*Avion III*) Apic/Contributor/Hulton Archive/Getty Images; p. 17 (zeppelin airship) Archive Photos/Stringer/Archive Photos/Getty Images; p. 17 (Lilienthal's glider) Fox Photos/Stringer/Hulton Archive/Getty Images; p. 17 (*Albatros*) World Imaging/Wikimedia Commons; p. 21 Alfred Eisenstaedt/Contributor/The LIFE Picture Collection/Getty Images; p. 22 Science & Society Picture Library/Contributor/SSPL/Getty Images; p. 23 Hulton Archive/Stringer/Archive Photos/Getty Images; p. 23 EclecticArkie/Wikimedia Commons; p. 25 Nina Leen/The LIFE Picture Collection/Getty Images; p. 27 Hans Meyer/Hulton Archive/Getty Images; p. 29 Flickr/Wikimedia Commons.

Printed in the United States of America

CPSIA compliance information: Batch #CS16GS: For further information contact Gareth Stevens, New York, New York at 1-800-542-2595.

CONTENTS

Words in the glossary appear in **bold** type
the first time they are used in the text.

A HISTORY OF INVENTING

Anyone can be an inventor. Over the course of human history, the curious and creative have invented all kinds of tools to make our lives better. An invention can be an improvement on something that exists already or something completely new! Inventions make the world what it is today. New kinds of eyeglasses, for example, have helped people see better than before. Computers and the Internet have changed how we communicate all over the world.

But not all inventions break new ground or last very long. Some are just plain freaky! And while inventors hope their ideas will serve a good purpose, many never make it very far. As you'll learn, some inventions can be downright dangerous and even kill their inventor!

SPECTACLES AND CASE FROM THE 1700s

PROTECT YOUR FACE

Inventions get freaky when they don't look like things we're used to seeing. For example, would you wear a clear plastic face shield that looks like a bird's beak? The face guard was meant to keep a person warm during winter by keeping the cold wind off their face. It might work better than a scarf, but does it look too freaky to use? The face gear even has a Dutch name that's a bit unusual: *plastic sneeuwstormbeschermer.*

THESE MASKS WERE WORN IN MONTREAL, CANADA, IN 1939. WOULD YOU WEAR ONE?

5

THE PERFORATION PADDLE

In the late 1800s, people didn't know what we know now about diseases and viruses. Yellow fever could kill someone within days of when they caught it, and people came up with many different ways to help stop it from spreading. That's why the perforation paddle was invented.

A perforation paddle had big spikes on it that perforated, or put holes, in mail so it could be **fumigated**. The mail—which people thought helped spread yellow fever—was then treated with chemicals, gases, or even acids in an effort to **decontaminate** it. Of course, none of this worked, and perforating the mail eventually stopped when doctors and scientists discovered that a virus was the real cause of yellow fever.

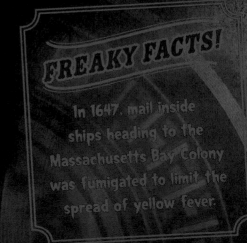

FREAKY FACTS!

In 1647, mail inside ships heading to the Massachusetts Bay Colony was fumigated to limit the spread of yellow fever.

YELLOW FEVER

Yellow fever is actually caused by a virus. It's passed to humans by mosquitoes. Yellow fever can kill within 4 to 8 days of being contracted, and symptoms of the disease include high fevers, headaches and backaches, and jaundice. Outbreaks were common in the 18th and 19th centuries. There's no known treatment for yellow fever, but a vaccination for the disease was developed by Dr. Max Theiler in 1939.

NO ONE REALIZED IT AT THE TIME, BUT MOSQUITOS LIKE THIS ONE ARE WHAT ACTUALLY CAUSE YELLOW FEVER TO SPREAD TO HUMANS.

PHONOGRAPH

Long before the digital music we download and listen to today, there was the phonograph. Though the phonograph machine looks strange to us today, it was an amazing invention when Thomas Edison created it in 1877. When Edison first introduced the phonograph to the public, it was so unexpected that people thought it was magical.

Other devices that could record sound were invented before the phonograph, but the phonograph was the first device that was able to play it back. The phonograph worked by using a **stylus**, which would trace grooves on a round disc called a record, reproducing the sound that was recorded. It was a **predecessor** to the record player, which itself is the predecessor of the compact disc. Your parents probably still have CDs lying around, and they may even have a record player!

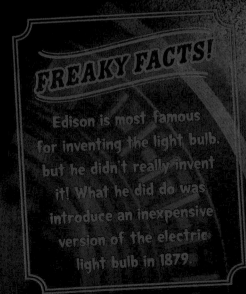

FREAKY FACTS!

Edison is most famous for inventing the light bulb, but he didn't really invent it! What he did do was introduce an inexpensive version of the electric light bulb in 1879.

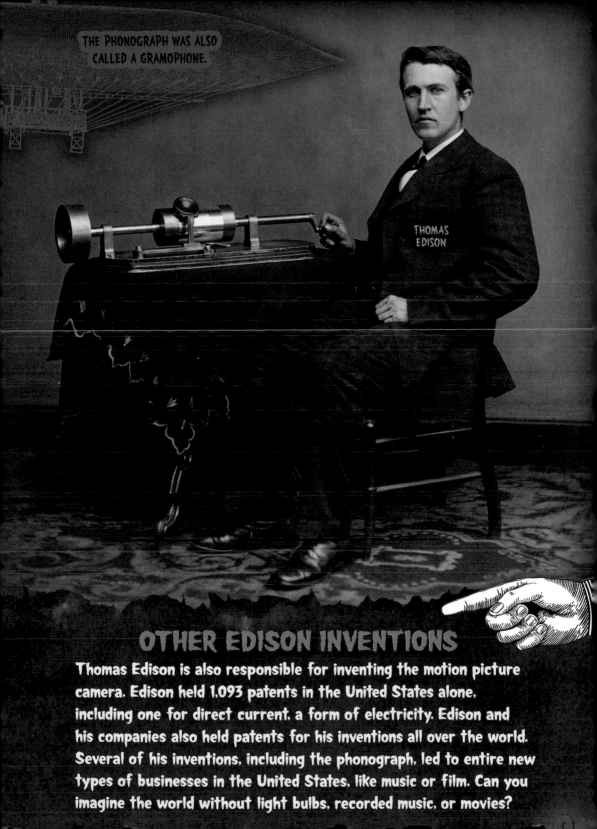

THE PHONOGRAPH WAS ALSO CALLED A GRAMOPHONE.

THOMAS EDISON

OTHER EDISON INVENTIONS

Thomas Edison is also responsible for inventing the motion picture camera. Edison held 1,093 patents in the United States alone, including one for direct current, a form of electricity. Edison and his companies also held patents for his inventions all over the world. Several of his inventions, including the phonograph, led to entire new types of businesses in the United States, like music or film. Can you imagine the world without light bulbs, recorded music, or movies?

LEPROSY CLAPPERS

Imagine having a disease so horrible, you'd have to let other people know you were coming so they could get away from you. It's a scary thought, isn't it? That's how it was for lepers in the 17th century. Leprosy clappers allowed people suffering from the disease to warn others they were coming near.

Leprosy was thought to be highly contagious, which means someone could get others sick by being close or touching them. Sufferers of the disease were often sent away by those living near them and had to live with other lepers. They may also have used the clappers to attract **benefactors** for gifts, as they were unable to make enough money to live on with the disease. There weren't many programs to help sick people in 17th-century England.

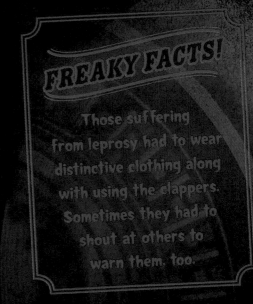

FREAKY FACTS!

Those suffering from leprosy had to wear distinctive clothing along with using the clappers. Sometimes they had to shout at others to warn them, too.

THESE WOODEN LEPROSY CLAPPERS WERE CARRIED BY PEOPLE WITH LEPROSY DURING THE 1600s IN ENGLAND.

LEPROSY

People were terrified of catching leprosy for good reason. It's a disease that attacks the nervous system and often leads to lumps on the skin, especially the face. People lose the ability to feel pain, which means they don't take care of wounds, leading to them losing limbs or getting major infections. While not common today, the disease is treated with medicine. Most of the cases occur in South America, Africa, and India.

MORTSAFE

During the 1800s, large numbers of students were going through England's medical schools to become doctors. But students needed human cadavers—or dead bodies—to practice on. At the time, giving a body to science was rare, and the only bodies available were those of executed criminals. The demand for bodies led to a rise in grave robbers, or people stealing buried bodies from cemeteries.

Enter the mortsafe. Invented around 1816, mortsafes were very heavy devices used to keep grave robbers away from bodies. Made of metal or stone, mortsafes were often put on top of coffins and could be taken off after a certain period of time. Some were actually metal cages that went around coffins in the ground.

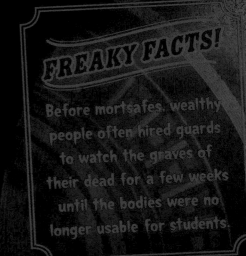

FREAKY FACTS!

Before mortsafes, wealthy people often hired guards to watch the graves of their dead for a few weeks until the bodies were no longer usable for students.

MORTSAFES BECAME POPULAR DURING THE 1800s AND CAN STILL BE FOUND IN SOME CEMETERIES AROUND THE UNITED KINGDOM.

MORTSAFE

TURNING A BLIND EYE

Grave robbing seems pretty freaky now, but it was big business for many. And grave robbers weren't chased by the police as often as you'd think. The need for bodies was so great, many officials ignored the incidents, even when mourning families complained. Officials also tried to keep word of the grave robbing quiet, so as to not upset others. Because when townspeople found out, riots, property damage, and even killings occurred over the practice.

STRANGE FLYING MACHINES

Today it's easy for people to take flight, but it took centuries of experiments and inventions to get there. The helicopters and airplanes we use today all have roots in some freaky flying machines. From strange wing contraptions to large flying machines, there are lots of different kinds.

One particularly strange flying machine was the Caproni CA-60 Noviplano. A cross between an airplane and a houseboat, the idea behind the strange, large contraption was that if it had enough wings, it would be able to sustain flight. Built in 1920, the aircraft had nine wings and weighed 55 tons (50 mt). Built to be the first **transatlantic** flying machine, the plane crashed after reaching 60 feet (18 m) in the air and was later burned.

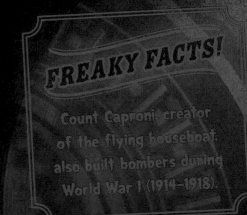

FREAKY FACTS!

Count Caproni, creator of the flying houseboat, also built bombers during World War I (1914–1918).

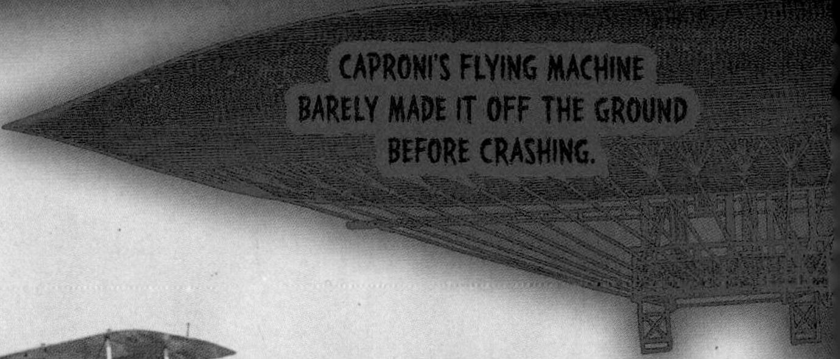

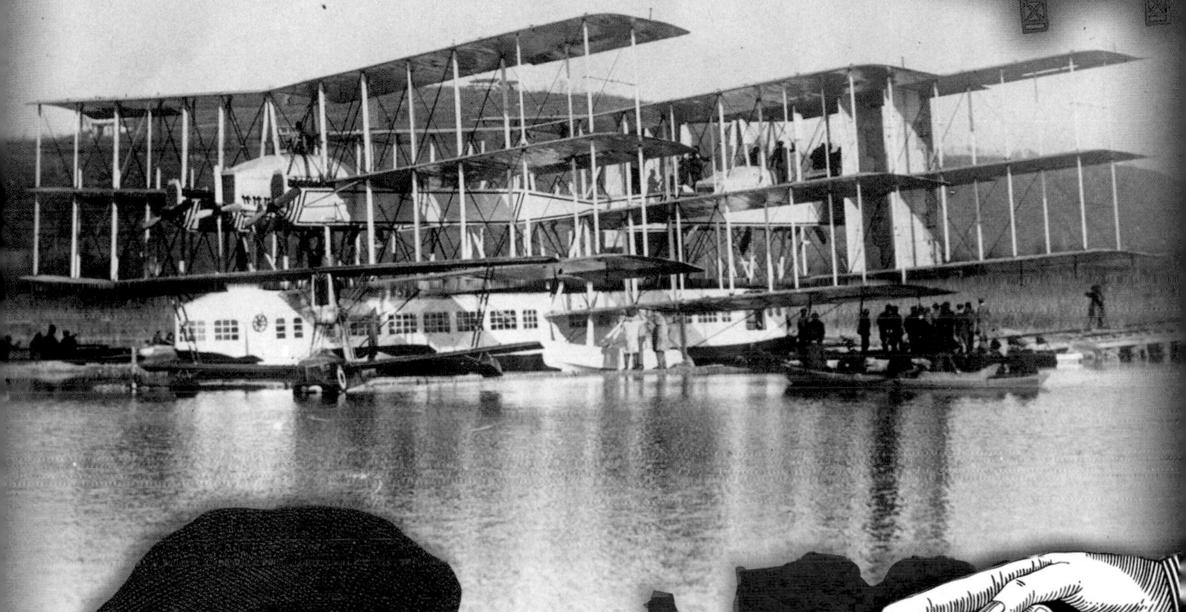

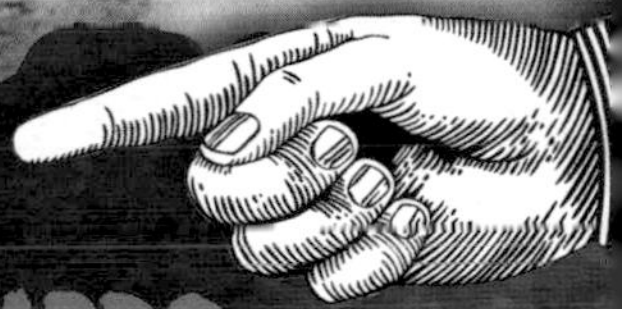

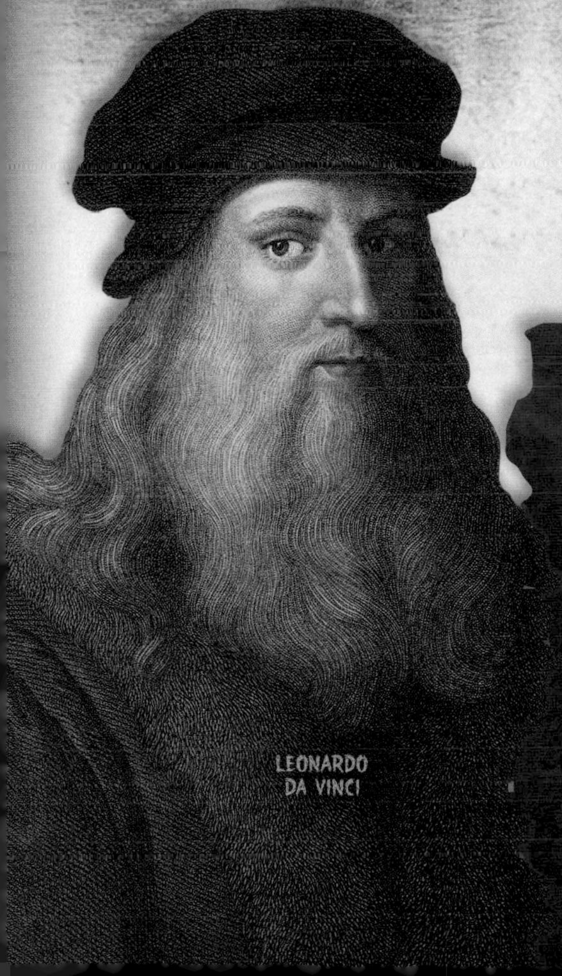

LEONARDO DA VINCI

Artist Leonardo da Vinci was fascinated by flight and studied birds to see how they flew. He designed several different types of flying machines, providing drawings and plans of his ideas. He even went so far as to build a model of a flying machine, although it never flew. It's not believed that da Vinci's drawings or models had any real impact on the airplanes that actually took flight, though.

LEONARDO
DA VINCI

15

In 1912, a French tailor named Franz Reichelt decided he was going to test out a "wingsuit" he designed that would be a wearable parachute for pilots. Reichelt lied to French police and said he was going to test the suit by putting a dummy inside it and drop it from the top of the Eiffel Tower in Paris, France. But when Reichelt arrived at the tower, he decided to jump himself.

Despite warnings from friends worried about the wind and the fact that the suit hadn't worked in other tests with dummies, Reichelt went ahead with the jump. He fell 187 feet (57 m) to his death. An **autopsy** later revealed that Reichelt had actually died during the fall. He had a heart attack!

FRANZ REICHELT

FREAKY FLYING MACHINES

JEAN-MARIE LE BRIS'
FLYING MACHINE ALBATROS II

OTTO LILIENTHAL'S
GLIDER

CLÉMENT ADER'S
FLYING MACHINE AVION III

ZEPPELIN AIRSHIP

OTHER DEADLY INVENTIONS

Franz Reichelt isn't the only inventor to die testing his invention. In 1903, 24-year-old William Nelson fell off the motorized bicycle he was testing out in New York, dying immediately. Max Valier invented rocket-powered cars and died in 1930 when an alcohol-fueled rocket exploded during a test. Thomas Midgely Jr. invented many different things, including the pulley system used to help him out of bed after he got polio. However, he got tangled in the ropes and died in 1944.

BEAUTY MICROMETER

Ever wonder how makeup artists figure out the right way to apply makeup to Hollywood stars? Well, in the 1930s, Max Factor Sr. developed the beauty micrometer. It was a strange-looking device that fit over a woman's head and showed a makeup artist any **imperfections** that needed to be fixed with makeup.

The mask, which was said to resemble an "instrument of torture" in a newspaper article, could be adjusted 325 ways to scientifically reveal so-called flaws of the face. The thinking behind the mask was that imperfections in an actress's face would show up much larger on the big screen. Factor imagined marketing the mask for use in beauty salons, but the freaky device never caught on outside of Hollywood.

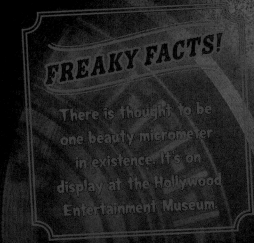

FREAKY FACTS!

There is thought to be one beauty micrometer in existence. It's on display at the Hollywood Entertainment Museum.

WHO'S MAX FACTOR?

Max Factor was a Polish **immigrant** who settled in St. Louis, Missouri, in the early 1900s. In 1908, he moved his family to Los Angeles, California, and began selling beauty products to the growing film industry. In 1914, he started developing makeup specifically made for actors and actresses. Criminals later tried to extort, or get money, out of Factor in Paris in 1938, and he died shortly after.

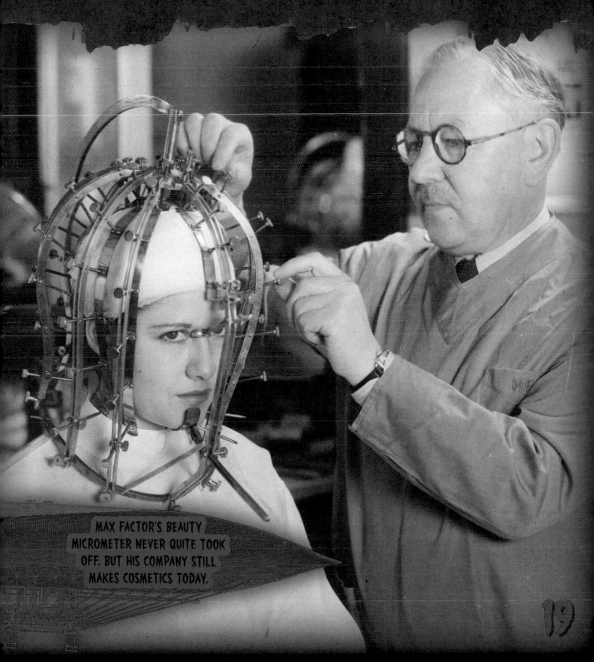

MAX FACTOR'S BEAUTY MICROMETER NEVER QUITE TOOK OFF, BUT HIS COMPANY STILL MAKES COSMETICS TODAY.

THE ISOLATOR

Have you ever had trouble concentrating? Maybe you're doing your homework and a little brother or sister is nagging you. Well, the Isolator was made for you. Developed in 1925, the Isolator was a strange helmet with oxygen piped in. The helmet blocked out noise and offered a tiny slit through which the wearer could see. Those using the helmet would only be able to see one line of text of whatever they were reading.

The helmet was invented by Hugo Gernsback, an early science fiction writer. It's unclear if the helmets were ever marketed or if anyone ever purchased one. Based on pictures, it's hard to believe anyone would actually wear one. What if someone needed to tell you something important?

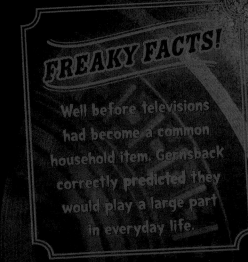

FREAKY FACTS!

Well before televisions had become a common household item, Gernsback correctly predicted they would play a large part in everyday life.

GERNSBACK USED MANY OF HIS INVENTIONS, INCLUDING HIS TV GLASSES, SHOWN HERE.

SCI-FI

Gernsback is such a big name in the world of science fiction literature that there's an award named after him: the Hugo Award, given to the top science fiction novel every year. Aside from inventing the bizarre helmet, Gernsback wrote and published many wild science fiction magazines. He also made predictions about the future. While he didn't see World War II or the Great Depression coming, he did correctly predict longer life-spans and curing childhood diseases like measles.

HEARING VOICES

Most people have cell phones these days, but what were phones like before we carried them around in our pockets? Alexander Graham Bell, a Scottish immigrant, invented what would become the modern phone in America in 1876. A lot has changed over the years, but the basic idea is the same: A phone gives you the ability to speak with people who aren't near you.

Early phones were large, boxy machines that looked quite a bit different from what we're used to now. In order to talk to someone back then, you had to connect to an operator, who would put you through to the person you were calling. Operators sat at big machines called switchboards and moved cables to connect different phone calls.

EDISON'S TELEPHONE

FREAKY FACTS!

Thomas Edison also invented a telephone he was able to patent!

OPERATORS FIRST HELPED SEND MESSAGES USING TELEGRAPHS, BUT BECAUSE OF LATER INVENTIONS THEY WERE SOON CONNECTING TELEPHONE CALLS USING SWITCHBOARDS.

INTERNATIONAL MORSE CODE
DISTRESS SIGNAL, SOS

TELE-WHAT?

Before the telephone, there was the telegraph machine. The telegraph allowed people to communicate over long distances using a system called Morse code. Because the technology to hear voices wasn't around just yet, telegraph operators had to know how to read the code coming across the telegraph wire. Different patterns of clicks represented different letters of the alphabet. Operators needed special training to quickly send and receive the code.

DIMPLE MACHINE

Do you have dimples? If you don't, do you want them? The dimple machine might have been able to help with that, although it might not have done anything at all. Isabella Gilbert invented the machine in 1936 in Rochester, New York. The device fit over the wearer's face, with two knobs pushing into the wearer's cheeks, one on each side. The idea behind the device was that it would train the cheeks into forming dimples.

However, it's unlikely the dimple machine worked. Dimples are actually created by muscles in our face. Still, people who want dimples today may try doing special exercises or pressing on their face to make them. There's no real proof any of it works, though.

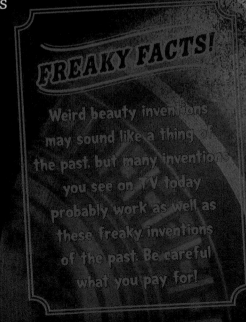

FREAKY FACTS!

Weird beauty inventions may sound like a thing of the past, but many inventions you see on TV today probably work as well as these freaky inventions of the past. Be careful what you pay for!

ANOTHER WILD BEAUTY INVENTION WAS THE PERMANENT WAVE MACHINE, WHICH WAS USED TO HELP PUT CURLS IN A WOMAN'S HAIR.

ALL FOR BEAUTY

Beauty inventions have often been a lot of talk and no results. Nose shapers were said to straighten or fix big or misshapen noses, while beauty masks promised to remove wrinkles. Masks and other mechanical devices promised to help people look younger, lose weight, and fix other problems. People would do anything to make themselves look better, including using extremely large hair dryers. There were even machines that promised to help grow a man's hair using heat and blue lights!

KIDS INVENTING

Plenty of kids have invented some freaky things for themselves. In 1996, 11-year-old Richie Stachowski realized there wasn't a good way for people to communicate when they're underwater. He thought up the "water talkie," which people could put on their mouth to talk underwater. The pool toy lets swimmers talk to one another from up to 15 feet (4.6 m) away!

A 12-year-old, Cassidy Goldstein, created crayon holders in 2002 after being frustrated with broken crayons that were too small to hold. Other kids' inventions are a bit more tasty. Frank Epperson was 11 in 1905 when he invented the popsicle! He left some soda powder in water and let it freeze overnight, creating an "Epsicle" he soon sold around his neighborhood.

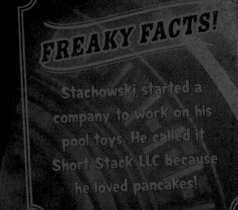

FREAKY FACTS!

Stachowski started a company to work on his pool toys. He called it Short Stack LLC because he loved pancakes!

FLOATING ON WATER

Ralph Samuelson was just 18 when he invented water skis, but other inventors found wacky ways to float on water. The Sea Suit was a nylon suit with air bubbles in it that helped the wearer float. You could lay back in the water and read or drink things without sinking. The whole family—even kids and the family dog—could wear it in the water!

THE SEA SUIT REALLY WORKED, BUT IT DIDN'T EXACTLY CATCH ON AS A POPULAR WAY TO FLOAT ON WATER.

WEIRD STUFF

People have come up with lots of freaky inventions over the years. In some cases, however, the reasons these things exist are simply lost to history. Take, for instance, the odd case of the gun camera showed off in New York City in 1938. All we know is that it was a handgun equipped with a camera. When the gun was fired, it took a picture. We don't know why it was invented, who invented it, or what purpose it served.

There's also the car from Paris, France, that was fitted with a shovel of sorts. The large device was said to scoop up pedestrians that were hit by the car, instead of just running them over. Maybe the inventor should have created something to help his driving instead!

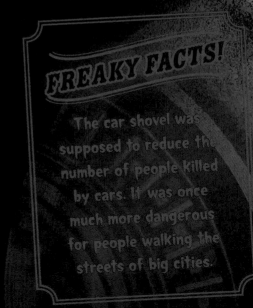

FREAKY FACTS!

The car shovel was supposed to reduce the number of people killed by cars. It was once much more dangerous for people walking the streets of big cities.

BUILD YOUR OWN

This book showed off a lot of silly-looking inventions, but don't be afraid to try your own hand at inventing something great. You might even have an idea that might improve an invention or make something new. If you come up with an idea, ask for help from an adult and give it a shot. Maybe you'll be the inventor of the next big thing. Who knows what the future holds for our inventions?

GLOSSARY

autopsy: to study a body to find out the cause of death

benefactor: a person who gives money or other help to a person or cause

decontaminate: to get rid of germs or things that spread illness

fumigate: to apply the fumes of certain chemicals to (an area) to rid it of germs or pests

immigrant: a person who comes to a new country to settle there

imperfection: a flaw or fault that makes something less than perfect

jaundice: a yellow coloring of the skin

predecessor: a thing that has been followed or replaced by another

predict: to guess about the future based on knowledge or experience

stylus: a small tool used for writing, marking, or navigating

symptom: a sign that shows someone is sick

transatlantic: crossing or moving across the Atlantic Ocean

FOR MORE INFORMATION

BOOKS

Higgins, Nadia. *The World's Oddest Inventions*. Mankato, MN: Capstone Press, 2015.

Houghton, Sarah. *Great Ideas and Where They Came From*. Mankato, MN: Capstone Curriculum Publishing, 2003.

Murphy, Jim. *Weird & Wacky Inventions*. New York City, NY: Sky Pony Press, 2011.

WEBSITES

10 Great Inventions Dreamt Up by Children
greatbusinessschools.org/10-great-inventions-dreamt-up-by-children/
Ever come up with your own inventions? Here are some things made by other kids!

27 of History's Strangest Inventions
brainpickings.org/2012/03/21/strange-invetions/
Check out some other strange inventions here.

INDEX